Elimination Play in Bridge

One of the first signs of maturity in a bridge player is a changed attitude towards finessing. Instead of running full tilt at every finesse in sight, he begins to adopt a more circumspect approach, looking for a way of making the contract even if the finesse is wrong.

The answer usually lies in elimination play, a weapon as superior to the finesse as is the rifle to the bow and arrow. In this book the authors explain exactly how it is done. With the aid of many brilliant examples covering a wide range of situations, they show how to eliminate the side suits, thus stripping an opponent of exit cards before throwing him in to make a fatal lead.

There is no more rewarding aspect of the game, and this introduction to elimination technique is calculated to set the average player upon the high road to expert country.

The authors have won equal distinction as players and as writers on the game. For many years Roger Trézel was an automatic choice for the French International Team, as was Terence Reese for the British. Both are European and World Champions.

'An excellent exposition of this rewarding stratagem'
—Pat Cotter, *Country Life*

D1336008

Terence Reese and Roger Trézel

Elimination Play in Bridge

LONDON
VICTOR GOLLANCZ LTD
in association with Peter Crawley
1986

First published in 1977 by Ward Lock Ltd

First published 1979 by Victor Gollancz Ltd,
14 Henrietta Street, London WC2E 8QJ
Second impression April 1979
Reissued 1986

© Terence Reese and Roger Trézel 1977

ISBN 0 575 02632 4

Printed in Great Britain by
St Edmundsbury Press Ltd, Bury St Edmunds, Suffolk

Introduction

by Terence Reese

The play of the cards at bridge is a big subject, capable of filling many large books. Some years ago Roger Trézel, the great French player and writer, had the idea of breaking up the game into several books of the present length, each dealing with one of the standard forms of technique. He judged, quite rightly as it turned out, that this scheme would appeal both to comparative beginners, who would be able to learn the game by stages, and to experienced players wishing to extend their knowledge of a particular branch of play.

We have now worked together on an English version, profiting from his experience.

Elimination Play

Of all forms of end-play elimination is the most frequent and the most rewarding. The object of the play is to force an opponent to make a lead that is disadvantageous for his side. Such a lead may save declarer from the necessity of taking a finesse, or it may allow him, in a suit contract, to discard a loser from one hand while he ruffs in the other.

It follows that *the opponent must not be allowed to retain a safe card of exit*. Elimination play is directed towards that end.

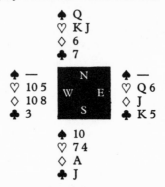

Spades are trumps and South, who has the lead, requires four of the last five tricks. If he simply finesses the jack of hearts, he will lose a heart and a club. But it is quite easy to circumvent one of these losers. South must first cash the ace of diamonds, *eliminating* East's card of exit. He follows with the jack of clubs, and East is in a classical dilemma: he must either lead a heart up to the K J, or a club, which will allow declarer to discard a heart and ruff in dummy.

It can be seen that playing off the ace of diamonds accomplishes two purposes: as the cards lie, it extracts the only diamond held by East; it also creates a situation in which, even if the defender who won the club trick held another diamond, he could not lead it safely. In the next example the declarer must eliminate a side suit from dummy and from his own hand before he throws the lead.

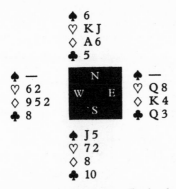

```
              ♠ 6
              ♡ K J
              ◇ A 6
              ♣ 5
♠ —                        ♠ —
♡ 6 2                      ♡ Q 8
◇ 9 5 2                    ◇ K 4
♣ 8                        ♣ Q 3
              ♠ J 5
              ♡ 7 2
              ◇ 8
              ♣ 10
```

Again spades are trumps, and South can afford to lose only one trick. He must begin by playing a diamond to the ace and ruffing a diamond, *eliminating* this suit from his own hand and dummy. Then a club, as before, leaves East on play.

In the majority of textbooks the term 'elimination play' is used only of situations that arise in a suit contract where the declarer has a trump in both hands at the moment of the throw-in. The defender may be forced to concede a ruff-and-discard. More often he will have the alternative of opening up a suit to his disadvantage. There may be a simple finesse, as in the example above, or any 'tenace position', such as A J x opposite 10 x x, where the prospects of losing only one trick are much improved if the defenders can be forced to lead the suit.

However, the elimination process also occurs in a no trump contract whenever the declarer executes a throw-in. The end-play will not succeed unless all safe cards of exit have been eliminated. So, our use of the term is not restricted to suit contracts: we give examples of elimination play in no trump contracts as well.

As you study the hands that follow, you will become familiar with several types of elimination. Before long you will see at a glance how to make contracts which, but for elimination play, would be impossible.

Example 1

You are South, playing four spades with the following cards:

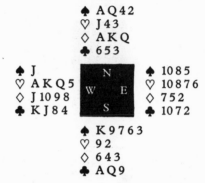

```
                    ♠ A Q 4 2
                    ♡ J 4 3
                    ◊ A K Q
                    ♣ 6 5 3
      ♠ J                              ♠ 10 8 5
      ♡ A K Q 5          N             ♡ 10 8 7 6
      ◊ J 10 9 8    W          E       ◊ 7 5 2
      ♣ K J 8 4          S             ♣ 10 7 2
                    ♠ K 9 7 6 3
                    ♡ 9 2
                    ◊ 6 4 3
                    ♣ A Q 9
```

West opens one heart, North doubles, and, after a pass by East, South jumps to two spades. North raises to three spades, and South bids the game.

The defenders begin with three rounds of hearts, South ruffing. Since the finesse of the queen of clubs is wrong, it may look as though two club tricks must be lost, but in fact South can make a certainty of the contract once everyone has followed to the first round of trumps.

After drawing trumps, South *eliminates* the diamonds by playing off ace, king and queen. Now dummy has the lead in this position.

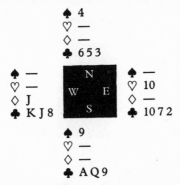

```
              ♠ 4
              ♡ —
              ◇ —
              ♣ 6 5 3
   ♠ —                      ♠ —
   ♡ —       N              ♡ 10
   ◇ J    W     E           ◇ —
   ♣ K J 8     S            ♣ 10 7 2
              ♠ 9
              ♡ —
              ◇ —
              ♣ A Q 9
```

Declarer leads a low club from the table. If East plays the two or the seven, South must not finesse the queen but must put in the nine. This leaves West with the alternative of returning a diamond, which will allow a ruff-and-discard, or a club up to the A Q.

Note that it will not avail East to insert the ten of clubs, because in that case the play of the queen will leave West in a similar dilemma. (It would, however, be good play for East to insert the ten; this would save the ship if South held A Q 8 of clubs and West, K J 9.)

Example 2

On the next hand declarer arrives at the same sort of ending after making an elimination play in two suits.

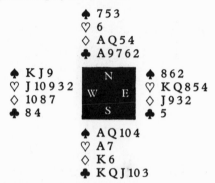

```
              ♠ 7 5 3
              ♡ 6
              ◇ A Q 5 4
              ♣ A 9 7 6 2
♠ K J 9                      ♠ 8 6 2
♡ J 10 9 3 2       N         ♡ K Q 8 5 4
◇ 10 8 7      W        E      ◇ J 9 3 2
♣ 8 4              S         ♣ 5
              ♠ A Q 10 4
              ♡ A 7
              ◇ K 6
              ♣ K Q J 10 3
```

Playing in six clubs, South wins the heart lead and draws trumps in two rounds. To escape the hazard of finding both spade honours in the wrong hand he sets about eliminating the red suits. First, he plays king, ace, and queen of diamonds, discarding a spade from hand; then he ruffs a fourth diamond. A heart ruff leaves him on the table with the remaining cards as follows:

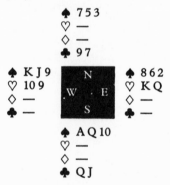

```
              ♠ 7 5 3
              ♡ —
              ◇ —
              ♣ 9 7
♠ K J 9                      ♠ 8 6 2
♡ 10 9            N          ♡ K Q
◇ —          W        E      ◇ —
♣ —               S          ♣ —
              ♠ A Q 10
              ♡ —
              ◇ —
              ♣ Q J
```

A low spade runs to the ten and jack, and West, stripped of all safe cards of exit, must either return a spade into the A Q or concede a ruff-and-discard.

Example 3

When it seems as though you will need a finesse for your contract, postpone that play until the last possible moment. Often you will find some means of avoiding it altogether.

Most elimination plays occur in suit contracts, but the same technique can be applied at no trumps, although in this case the ruff-and-discard element is not present. Here, the declarer in three no trumps made several attempts to find his ninth trick, but they all failed because his technique was deficient.

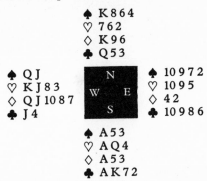

```
              ♠ K 8 6 4
              ♡ 7 6 2
              ◇ K 9 6
              ♣ Q 5 3
♠ Q J              N              ♠ 10 9 7 2
♡ K J 8 3                         ♡ 10 9 5
◇ Q J 10 8 7   W       E          ◇ 4 2
♣ J 4              S              ♣ 10 9 8 6
              ♠ A 5 3
              ♡ A Q 4
              ◇ A 5 3
              ♣ A K 7 2
```

South opened two no trumps and was raised to three no trumps. West led the queen of diamonds, and South saw no reason not to capture the first trick with the ace.

There were eight tricks on top and the chances for a ninth included a 3-3 break in spades, a 3-3 break in clubs, and a finesse of the queen of hearts.

Keeping his powder dry, as he put it to himself, South tested the spades first, leading low from hand. When West played the jack, South let him hold the trick.

West followed with the jack of diamonds, and South deemed this a suitable moment to hold up the king. That was his big mistake.

West played a third round of diamonds on which East discarded a heart. South played three rounds of clubs, finding this suit 4-2, then tested the spades, but these also did not break evenly. Muttering 'Not my day', South resorted finally to the heart finesse and was not surprised when this lost also. West thereupon cashed two diamonds to defeat the contract.

Here, South failed to retain a *card of exit*. He should have won the second diamond and tested the black suits, as before. When they proved recalcitrant, he could exit with the nine of diamonds, forcing West, after he had cashed his diamond winners, to lead away from the king of hearts.

Example 4

There are two ways of looking at a finesse. On the one hand, it is attractive to win a trick that might be lost; on the other, it is undesirable to take a chance that might be avoided.

Any player who regards a finesse not with fascination, but with misgiving, is half-way to becoming a good player, even if he does not at first discover the best means to avoid the hazard; this knowledge will come with practice.

Here you are South in a contract of six diamonds.

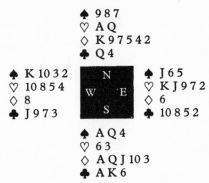

```
              ♠ 9 8 7
              ♡ A Q
              ◇ K 9 7 5 4 2
              ♣ Q 4
  ♠ K 10 3 2              ♠ J 6 5
  ♡ 10 8 5 4      N       ♡ K J 9 7 2
  ◇ 8          W     E    ◇ 6
  ♣ J 9 7 3       S       ♣ 10 8 5 2
              ♠ A Q 4
              ♡ 6 3
              ◇ A Q J 10 3
              ♣ A K 6
```

South opens one diamond, and North has nothing better than to give a double raise to three diamonds. From this point South will not stop short of six diamonds.

West's lead of the four of hearts presents South with an immediate problem. Players quite often underlead a king against a small slam, so the finesse may hold; and if it fails, a spade can be discarded on the third club, and a finesse of the spade queen will win the contract. In short, South appears to need one finesse out of two, which is a 75% chance, if one regards each finesse as an even proposition.

Thanks, however, to the presence of the 9 8 7 of spades on the table, South can make a certainty of the contract by a different line of play. He should go up with the ace of hearts, draw trumps, and take three rounds of clubs, discarding the queen of hearts from dummy. A heart is ruffed and the position is:

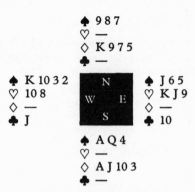

♠ 9 8 7
♡ —
♢ K 9 7 5
♣ —

♠ K 10 3 2   ♠ J 6 5
♡ 10 8   ♡ K J 9
♢ —   ♢ —
♣ J   ♣ 10

♠ A Q 4
♡ —
♢ A J 10 3
♣ —

Now South can laugh at fate. He leads a spade from dummy and
covers any higher card played by East. West will win this trick but
will have no good return.

Example 5

Sometimes you will aim to lose a trick to a particular opponent, because no lead by that player will present an immediate danger; that is a sensible precaution. Sometimes the surrender of a trick to a particular opponent will force him to give up a trick, whatever he returns; then you have a perfect safety play. On the deal below you achieve this result by means of an elimination followed by a classic 'loser-on-loser' play.

```
            ♠ J 4 3
            ♡ 6 5 2
            ◊ K Q 8 4
            ♣ K 4 2
♠ 9 5                      ♠ 7 2
♡ A J 3         N          ♡ Q 10 9 8
◊ J 10 7 6   W     E       ◊ 9 2
♣ Q J 10 8      S          ♣ A 9 6 5 3
            ♠ A K Q 10 8 6
            ♡ K 7 4
            ◊ A 5 3
            ♣ 7
```

South plays in four spades, and West leads the queen of clubs. It would, of course, be poor play to cover with the king, forcing East to take the trick and giving him a chance to lead a heart through the king. South plays low from dummy, therefore, and probably East will play low as well, although, as the cards lie, the winning defence is to overtake. West follows with the jack of clubs, and South ruffs. The trumps fall in two rounds, and at this point South can be sure of the contract if the ace of hearts is held by East, or if the diamonds are 3-3, permitting him to discard a heart on dummy's long diamond.

There is an additional chance, however, which will ensure the contract not only if diamonds are 3-3 but also if West holds four or more. Declarer plays off ace and king of diamonds, ruffs the king of clubs, and leads a third diamond, arriving at this position:

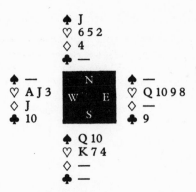

Now the four of diamonds is led from dummy, and South discards the four of hearts. West takes this trick and is forced to return a heart or a club, either of which will present declarer with his tenth trick.

Example 6

To land a contract of five clubs doubled against an opponent who has the values for an opening two no trumps is a satisfactory achievement, all the more so when the distribution is not abnormal, and the contract has been reached by way of a delicate auction.

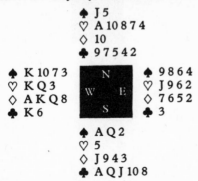

```
                    ♠ J 5
                    ♡ A 10 8 7 4
                    ◇ 10
                    ♣ 9 7 5 4 2
  ♠ K 10 7 3                      ♠ 9 8 6 4
  ♡ K Q 3           N             ♡ J 9 6 2
  ◇ A K Q 8      W     E          ◇ 7 6 5 2
  ♣ K 6             S             ♣ 3
                    ♠ A Q 2
                    ♡ 5
                    ◇ J 9 4 3
                    ♣ A Q J 10 8
```

South was the dealer at love all and the bidding went:

SOUTH	WEST	NORTH	EAST
1 ♣	dble	1 ♡	pass
1 NT	dble	2 ♣	pass
3 ♣	3 ◇	pass	pass
dble	pass	4 ♣	pass
5 ♣	dble	pass	pass
pass			

When North took out the double of three diamonds, it was reasonable to suppose that he was short of this suit, and this encouraged South to bid the game. Most players would have doubled five clubs, as West did, but it is worth remarking that an expert would have refrained from doing so: he would have realized that the double stood to gain only an extra 50, at most, and that the defence might prove difficult.

West led the king of diamonds and switched to the king of hearts, hoping eventually to make a spade, a diamond, and a club. South won with the ace of hearts, ruffed a heart, and led the jack of diamonds, forcing West to cover. Dummy ruffed, and after another heart had been ruffed, South played off ace and another club. West found himself on lead in this position:

17

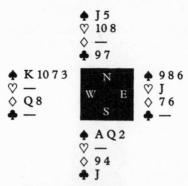

```
              ♠ J 5
              ♡ 10 8
              ◇ —
              ♣ 9 7

♠ K 10 7 3      N        ♠ 9 8 6
♡ —          W      E     ♡ J
◇ Q 8           S        ◇ 7 6
♣ —                      ♣ —

              ♠ A Q 2
              ♡ —
              ◇ 9 4
              ♣ J
```

South was still a trick short on the surface, but whatever West played was bound to give him the extra trick he needed. West in fact led a low diamond, hoping that South would not play him for the queen. South was not deceived, however; he let the eight run to his nine, discarding a spade from dummy, ruffed a diamond, ruffed a heart, cashed the ace of spades, and made the last two tricks with dummy's last trump and the established ten of hearts. It was neatly done, and the hand is worth playing over again.

Example 7

The play on the deal below is similar to that of Example 5. It is only by observing several hands of the same type that you will acquire the facility to bring off a similar coup at the table.

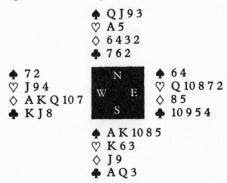

```
              ♠ Q J 9 3
              ♡ A 5
              ◇ 6 4 3 2
              ♣ 7 6 2
♠ 7 2                        ♠ 6 4
♡ J 9 4          N          ♡ Q 10 8 7 2
◇ A K Q 10 7   W   E        ◇ 8 5
♣ K J 8          S          ♣ 10 9 5 4
              ♠ A K 10 8 5
              ♡ K 6 3
              ◇ J 9
              ♣ A Q 3
```

South opens one spade, West doubles, and North jumps to three spades, making it too dangerous for East to enter. Although he recognizes his partner's jump as a defensive measure, South decides that he is strong enough to bid the game.

West leads the king of diamonds against four spades and follows with ace and another. South ruffs and is happy to find the trumps 2-2, for now he has a cast-iron loser-on-loser elimination. He ruffs the third round of hearts in dummy to eliminate this suit and the remaining cards are:

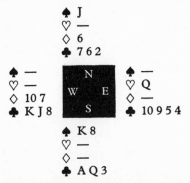

```
              ♠ J
              ♡ —
              ◇ 6
              ♣ 7 6 2
♠ —                         ♠ —
♡ —             N          ♡ Q
◇ 10 7        W   E         ◇ —
♣ K J 8         S          ♣ 10 9 5 4
              ♠ K 8
              ♡ —
              ◇ —
              ♣ A Q 3
```

Now South does not expose himself to the hazard of the club finesse. Instead, he leads the losing diamond from dummy and discards the three of clubs from hand. West, left on lead, must either return a club or concede a ruff-and-discard.

Example 8

Quite often a hand that would be lay-down against normal distribution will become a problem because of an unexpected break. It is very much a part of expert play to foresee the possibility of bad breaks and to take counter-measures in good time.

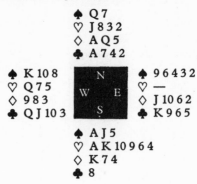

```
                    ♠ Q 7
                    ♡ J 8 3 2
                    ◇ A Q 5
                    ♣ A 7 4 2
   ♠ K 10 8                      ♠ 9 6 4 3 2
   ♡ Q 7 5                       ♡ —
   ◇ 9 8 3                       ◇ J 10 6 2
   ♣ Q J 10 3                    ♣ K 9 6 5
                    ♠ A J 5
                    ♡ A K 10 9 6 4
                    ◇ K 7 4
                    ♣ 8
```

South is in six hearts, and West leads the queen of clubs, taken by dummy's ace. Without a care in the world South plays a heart to the ace. Harmless as it may seem, this play costs declarer the contract. Sooner or later he will lose a trump and a spade.

An expert player would sum up the hand like this:

'The slam is cold unless West has three hearts to the queen and the king of spades. If that is the situation, what can I do about it?

'Perhaps I can lose the trump trick at a moment when West has only spades left and will be forced to lead away from the king. To bring about that situation I must prepare to eliminate the clubs and diamonds. Dummy has only a limited number of entries, so I had better begin by ruffing a club.'

Observe the effect of ruffing a club at trick two. When the ace of hearts reveals the trump distribution, South plays a diamond to the queen, ruffs a club, cashes the king of hearts, plays a diamond to the ace, and ruffs the last club. All follow to the king of diamonds, and the position is now:

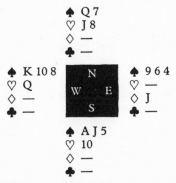

South exists with his last trump, and West is obliged to lead a spade.

This is not a 'perfect elimination', because West might have held a safe card of exit at the finish; for example, he might have held a spade fewer and an extra diamond or club. Even so, the elimination would have cost nothing. Dummy would ruff the next lead, and the spade finesse would still be available.

Example 9

The next example might be classified by some writers as a trump coup rather than an elimination deal, but the elimination process is an essential part of the play, however one describes it.

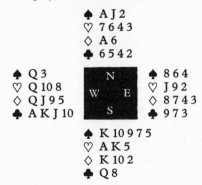

♠ A J 2
♡ 7 6 4 3
◇ A 6
♣ 6 5 4 2

♠ Q 3
♡ Q 10 8
◇ Q J 9 5
♣ A K J 10

♠ 8 6 4
♡ J 9 2
◇ 8 7 4 3
♣ 9 7 3

♠ K 10 9 7 5
♡ A K 5
◇ K 10 2
♣ Q 8

North-South reached a borderline contract of four spades by this route:

SOUTH	WEST	NORTH	EAST
1 ♠	dble	redble	pass
pass	2 ♣	2 ♠	pass
3 ♠	pass	4 ♠	pass
pass	pass		

West began with three rounds of clubs, South ruffing. There was no way to escape a heart loser, and the contract appeared to depend on the trump finesse. As West had doubled the opening bid, he might well have a singleton spade, but this was by no means certain.

South decided, however, that there was no need to meet this problem head on. If he could eliminate the side suits, then exit with his losing heart, he might avoid the spade guess altogether.

After ruffing the third club, therefore, South cashed the ace and king of hearts, played three rounds of diamonds, ruffing on the table, then led the fourth club from dummy. The remaining cards were:

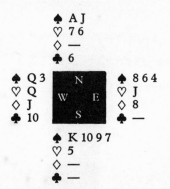

♠ A J
♡ 7 6
♢ —
♣ 6

♠ Q 3   ♠ 8 6 4
♡ Q   ♡ J
♢ J   ♢ 8
♣ 10   ♣ —

♠ K 10 9 7
♡ 5
♢ —
♣ —

When East showed out on the club, the contract was guaranteed.
South ruffed with the seven of spades and exited with his heart; he
was now in the comfortable position of holding K 10 9 of spades
opposite A J, with the opponents in the lead.

Example 10

As a means of recording your progress, see if you can form a plan that will make certain of a contract of five diamonds on the deal below. It will be a better test, obviously, if you refrain from looking at the East-West cards. The opening lead by West is the king of hearts, and all follow to the first round of trumps.

```
              ♠ A K
              ♡ A J
              ◇ K 9 7 6 3
              ♣ 7 5 4 3
  ♠ J 9 6 2                    ♠ Q 10 8 5 4
  ♡ K Q 10 8        N          ♡ 9 7 6 5
  ◇ 5           W       E      ◇ 8 4 2
  ♣ Q 10 9 2        S          ♣ 6
              ♠ 7 3
              ♡ 4 3 2
              ◇ A Q J 10
              ♣ A K J 8
```

It is correct to draw three rounds of trumps. The last thing you must do now is finesse the jack of clubs. Instead, you begin the elimination process by exiting with a heart to West's queen. West will probably lead a spade, which you take in dummy. You play a club to the ace, ruff the third heart, and cash the king of spades. The position is now:

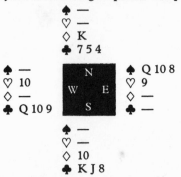

```
              ♠ —
              ♡ —
              ◇ K
              ♣ 7 5 4
  ♠ —                          ♠ Q 10 8
  ♡ 10              N          ♡ 9
  ◇ —           W       E      ◇ —
  ♣ Q 10 9          S          ♣ —
              ♠ —
              ♡ —
              ◇ 10
              ♣ K J 8
```

You lead a low club from the table. If East follows suit, you can finesse the jack, but when East shows void, you put in the eight of clubs, leaving West on play.

It is worth noting that, even if you are in your own hand, you can ensure the contract by exiting with a low club; whether West or East has the remaining clubs you will make the rest of the tricks.

24

1ST JULY 2000

AN AESTHETIC ERROR (?)

At TRICK 4 dealer should ruff
with the ACE, lead the JACK to
dummy's QUEEN of SPADES, ruff
the last DIAMOND with the
KING OF TRUMPS and then cross
to DUMMY in trumps again
(drawing the last trump from
EAST)

The 9 HEARTS is led and the
6 CLUBS discarded.
WEST is caught in a PERFECT

Example 11

We have seen two examples already (5 and 7) of loser-on-loser play. The next hand shows a double loser-on-loser; at the same time the declarer establishes an additional winner.

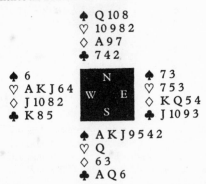

```
              ♠ Q 10 8
              ♡ 10 9 8 2
              ◇ A 9 7
              ♣ 7 4 2
♠ 6                           ♠ 7 3
♡ A K J 6 4       N           ♡ 7 5 3
◇ J 10 8 2    W       E       ◇ K Q 5 4
♣ K 8 5           S           ♣ J 10 9 3
              ♠ A K J 9 5 4 2
              ♡ Q
              ◇ 6 3
              ♣ A Q 6
```

West leads the king of hearts against South's contract of four spades. When he sees the queen drop, West switches to the jack of diamonds, which is won in dummy.

It looks on the surface as though South must lose a heart, a diamond, and one or two clubs, depending on the position of the king. However, the reader will have learned to distrust finesses by now. What alternative exists?

Like a chef who makes use of the 'bits and pieces', declarer must build a trick from dummy's 10 9 8 of hearts. His first move, after winning with the ace of diamonds, is to lead the ten of hearts and discard his losing diamond. West wins and will probably exit with a diamond, which South will ruff.

Now two rounds of spades are taken to eliminate East's trumps. That leaves:

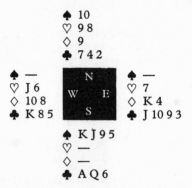

```
              ♠ 10
              ♡ 9 8
              ◇ 9
              ♣ 7 4 2
♠ —                        ♠ —
♡ J 6      N              ♡ 7
◇ 10 8   W    E           ◇ K 4
♣ K 8 5     S             ♣ J 10 9 3
              ♠ K J 9 5
              ♡ —
              ◇ —
              ♣ A Q 6
```

South plays the nine of hearts from dummy and again discards a loser, the six of clubs. West wins with the jack and exits with a diamond. South ruffs, crosses to the ten of spades, and discards the queen of clubs on the established eight of hearts.

The elimination factor was not prominent on this deal, but the general purpose of the play was the same as in most elimination hands—to find a way to avoid a risky finesse. There are three points to notice in the play:

1) South's first discard must be a diamond, not a club. If he discards a club, West will play a diamond to his partner's queen, and East will lead a club through the A Q before South has established the heart winner.

2) South must not draw two rounds of trumps early on, because then he will be short of an entry to dummy at the finish.

3) South must, however, draw trumps before leading the third round of hearts. If he fails to do so, West will win with the jack and play a fourth round, killing the winner in dummy.

Example 12

Anyone can play off aces and kings and win the finesses that are right. The difficult art is to win the finesses that are wrong. Observe how South, on the deal below, discovers a slight extra chance.

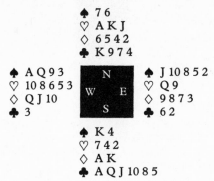

```
              ♠ 7 6
              ♡ A K J
              ◇ 6 5 4 2
              ♣ K 9 7 4
♠ A Q 9 3         N          ♠ J 10 8 5 2
♡ 10 8 6 5 3   W     E        ♡ Q 9
◇ Q J 10          S          ◇ 9 8 7 3
♣ 3                           ♣ 6 2
              ♠ K 4
              ♡ 7 4 2
              ◇ A K
              ♣ A Q J 10 8 5
```

South plays in five clubs, although three no trumps would be somewhat easier.

West leads the queen of diamonds, taken by South's ace. The contract is safe unless both the queen of hearts and the ace of spades lie badly for the declarer. If you have stolen a look at the defending hands, you will have seen that both cards are, in fact, 'wrong', but the queen of hearts is doubleton. South cannot know this, but if he plays his cards in the right sequence he will, nevertheless, drop the queen.

After winning with the ace of diamonds, South draws trumps, cashes the king of diamonds, enters dummy with a heart, and ruffs a diamond. Then he plays a trump to the table and eliminates the fourth diamond. He has arrived at this position:

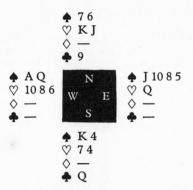

South leads a heart towards dummy and goes up with the king, dropping East's queen. If East gives him an old-fashioned look, as though to say 'Was I holding my cards in the middle of the table?', South has a ready answer:

'If West has the queen of hearts, I make the contract anyway, because when he wins the next round of hearts, he will have to lead a spade or give me a ruff-and-discard. If you (East) have the queen of hearts guarded, it makes no difference whether I take the king now or finesse. I was playing for the extra chance that the queen might be doubleton.'

Note that, to bring about this situation, South had to eliminate the diamonds from dummy; otherwise, he would have no good reason to spurn the heart finesse.

Example 13

As most players know from experience, a borderline contract of three no trumps tends to be easier to make when there has been an opening bid by an opponent than when there has been no bidding. This is partly because the same hand has to win tricks and lead away from strength all the time, and partly because declarer is able to place the high cards with fair certainty. Both factors assisted South on the following deal, but he also needed to play with good technique.

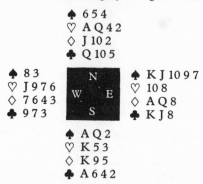

```
              ♠ 6 5 4
              ♡ A Q 4 2
              ◇ J 10 2
              ♣ Q 10 5
  ♠ 8 3                      ♠ K J 10 9 7
  ♡ J 9 7 6        N         ♡ 10 8
  ◇ 7 6 4 3    W.     E      ◇ A Q 8
  ♣ 9 7 3          S         ♣ K J 8
              ♠ A Q 2
              ♡ K 5 3
              ◇ K 9 5
              ♣ A 6 4 2
```

South played in three no trumps after East had opened the bidding with one spade. West led the eight of spades, and East covered with the nine.

The normal play, with A Q x of the suit led, would be to hold up, so that if West held a doubleton and won the first defensive trick, perhaps with the king of clubs or the queen of diamonds, he would not have a second spade to lead. However, South does not expect West to gain the lead at any time. (True, there is room for East to have an opening bid and West to hold the queen of diamonds, but South really needs to assume that the diamond finesse is right.)

South sees no point in holding up, therefore, especially as he may need the third spade later on as a card of exit. He will have to take the diamond finesse sooner or later, so he enters dummy with the queen of hearts and leads the jack of diamonds. East goes up with the ace (a play that confirms his possession of the queen) and leads the king of spades.

Still more now there could be no advantage in holding up the ace. Having won this trick, South tests the hearts, East discarding the eight of clubs on the third round. A low diamond is won by the nine, and declarer is now in pretty good shape, with these cards remaining:

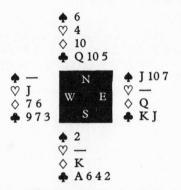

```
              ♠ 6
              ♡ 4
              ◇ 10
              ♣ Q 10 5
    ♠ —                      ♠ J 10 7
    ♡ J        N             ♡ —
    ◇ 7 6   W     E          ◇ Q
    ♣ 9 7 3     S            ♣ K J
              ♠ 2
              ♡ —
              ◇ K
              ♣ A 6 4 2
```

Having a good picture of the distribution, South eliminates East's last diamond by cashing the king and then exits with a spade. After making his three spade tricks, East has to lead a club away from the king. South loses just one diamond and three spades.

There were two critical moves in the play. First, South had to retain a low spade as a card of exit (compare Example 3). Second, he had to risk cashing the king of diamonds at the finish in order to strip East of his third diamond. It is worth remarking that this type of end-play, in a no trump contract, tends not to be such a sure thing as a similar end-play in a suit contract. It was just possible, here, that East had begun with four diamonds and two clubs and had cleverly bared his king of clubs quite early in the play.

Example 14

End-plays at no trumps sometimes depend on making a reasonable assumption, as in the hand above, but sometimes declarer can be quite certain of the distribution. Here is a typical hand where South can get a count of every suit.

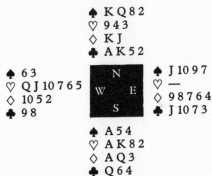

```
                  ♠ K Q 8 2
                  ♡ 9 4 3
                  ◇ K J
                  ♣ A K 5 2
    ♠ 6 3                        ♠ J 10 9 7
    ♡ Q J 10 7 6 5      N         ♡ —
    ◇ 10 5 2        W       E     ◇ 9 8 7 6 4
    ♣ 9 8               S         ♣ J 10 7 3
                  ♠ A 5 4
                  ♡ A K 8 2
                  ◇ A Q 3
                  ♣ Q 6 4
```

South plays in six no trumps, and West leads the queen of hearts. East discards a low diamond, and South wins with the king of hearts.

There are eleven tricks on top and declarer has nothing better than to take three top spades, followed by three top clubs. He finds a 4-2 break in each suit.

No squeeze is possible, because both suits are guarded by East, who discards after North. In technical terms the two 'menaces', the fourth spade and the fourth club, are unfavourably placed.

The only hope lies in a throw-in, and here the picture is brighter. West is known to hold six hearts, two clubs, and two spades. He can be end-played in hearts, but first it is necessary to extract his diamonds. South takes three rounds of diamonds, therefore, arriving at this position:

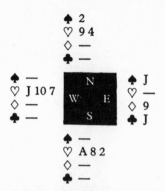

South leads the two of hearts, West plays the ten, and South is careful to unblock with dummy's nine. Then West is forced to return a heart into the A 8.

When this hand was given to a class of pupils, one of them found an odd way to go down at the finish. Instead of keeping the nine and four of hearts and a black card in dummy, he came down to the nine of hearts alone, a spade, and a club. When a low heart was led, West, by accident or design, played low; dummy's nine won, but the defence took the last two tricks.

Example 15

Players who make light overcalls often do not realize how much help they give to an astute declarer. East's overcall on the deal below, plus an inconspicuous error by West in the play, enabled South to bring home a vulnerable slam.

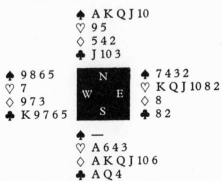

After a pass by West, North opened one spade, and East overcalled with two hearts. Most players would have done the same, but East really had no chance to fight for the contract. As it was, South quickly arrived at six diamonds.

West led the seven of hearts to his partner's ten and declarer's ace. Had there been no adverse bidding, South would surely have tried to enter dummy with a heart ruff, and this would not have been a success. Warned by the opening bid, and judging the lead to be a singleton, South adopted a different plan. He played off the ace and king of diamonds, then exited with the six of diamonds, forcing West to take the trick. West tried a club, and now there was an entry to dummy's spade suit.

Did anyone make a mistake? Yes, indeed, and West was the first to comment on it:

'I ought to have unblocked the seven and nine of diamonds,' he said, much mortified.

Example 16

To achieve a successful throw-in a declarer must do two things: he must eliminate the side suits, as we have seen on several occasions, and he must also make sure that he loses the critical trick to the 'right' defender. This may call for skilful manoeuvring.

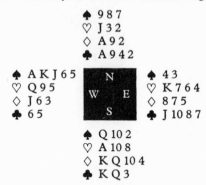

```
              ♠ 9 8 7
              ♡ J 3 2
              ◇ A 9 2
              ♣ A 9 4 2
♠ A K J 6 5                    ♠ 4 3
♡ Q 9 5         N             ♡ K 7 6 4
◇ J 6 3       W   E           ◇ 8 7 5
♣ 6 5           S             ♣ J 10 8 7
              ♠ Q 10 2
              ♡ A 10 8
              ◇ K Q 10 4
              ♣ K Q 3
```

Defending against three no trumps, West does not want to give away a cheap trick to the queen of spades, so he leads the ace, conventionally asking his partner to drop an honour or to play high-low from a doubleton. When East follows with the four and South the ten, West rightly concludes that South has false-carded from Q 10 x, so he switches to the six of clubs.

With only seven tricks on top South begins by taking three rounds of clubs, West discarding a diamond on the third round. It is likely now that the diamonds will produce four tricks, and South might reasonably look for his ninth trick in hearts. He could take a deep finesse of the eight; if this forced the king or queen, he could finesse the ten on the next round.

There is a stronger line, however, which most players would miss. Preparing for an end-play against West (whom he places with A K J of spades), South should lead the jack of hearts from dummy. East must cover, for otherwise the jack will run to the queen, and a subsequent finesse of the ten will produce the ninth trick. After the jack of hearts has been covered by the king and ace, declarer turns to diamonds, reaching this position:

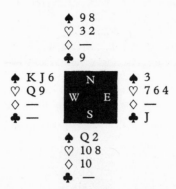

```
                ♠ 9 8
                ♡ 3 2
                ◇ —
                ♣ 9
    ♠ K J 6              ♠ 3
    ♡ Q 9       N        ♡ 7 6 4
    ◇ —     W     E      ◇ —
    ♣ —         S        ♣ J
                ♠ Q 2
                ♡ 10 8
                ◇ 10
                ♣ —
```

Obviously West is in trouble when the last diamond is led. If he discards a spade, then South should exit in spades, in case East has the nine of hearts.

This is an instructive hand in many ways. Note the lead of the ace of spades in preference to fourth best; East's play of the four from a doubleton (some players follow a different system, playing the top card from three); South's false card of the ten of spades, in an attempt to suggest a doubleton Q 10; and the lead of the jack of hearts from dummy, with the basic idea of leaving West in control of the next round of hearts.

Example 17

Declarer's problem on the last hand was to throw the lead to the right player at the right time. On the deal below the problem is to ensure that when West is thrown in he will have no safe card of exit. This calls for careful timing in the play of the side suits.

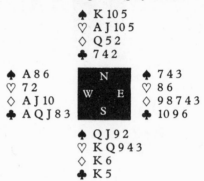

```
                    ♠ K 10 5
                    ♡ A J 10 5
                    ◇ Q 5 2
                    ♣ 7 4 2
     ♠ A 8 6                        ♠ 7 4 3
     ♡ 7 2          N               ♡ 8 6
     ◇ A J 10    W     E            ◇ 9 8 7 4 3
     ♣ A Q J 8 3    S               ♣ 10 9 6
                    ♠ Q J 9 2
                    ♡ K Q 9 4 3
                    ◇ K 6
                    ♣ K 5
```

The bidding goes:

SOUTH	WEST	NORTH	EAST
1 ♡	dble	2 NT	pass
4 ♡	pass	pass	pass

North's two no trumps, over the double, conventionally shows a 'genuine', as opposed to a 'pre-emptive', raise to three hearts. Thus encouraged, South must bid the game, as three hearts by him would be a sign-off.

West leads a trump, and after two rounds of hearts, declarer plays on spades. West captures the second round and exits with a third spade. This leaves:

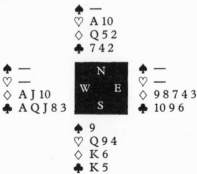

```
                    ♠ —
                    ♡ A 10
                    ◇ Q 5 2
                    ♣ 7 4 2
     ♠ —                            ♠ —
     ♡ —            N               ♡ —
     ◇ A J 10    W     E            ◇ 9 8 7 4 3
     ♣ A Q J 8 3    S               ♣ 10 9 6
                    ♠ 9
                    ♡ Q 9 4
                    ◇ K 6
                    ♣ K 5
```

Oddly enough—and this is not easy to see at first—it would be a mistake to cash the last spade at this point. Instead, South must lead a low diamond from hand. This places West in a dilemma. If he goes up with the ace, he presents the declarer with two diamond tricks, so for the moment he must play the ten. Declarer wins with the queen, returns to hand with the queen of hearts, and only then plays the thirteenth spade, discarding a *diamond* from dummy. Then he exits with the king of diamonds, and West is left with the alternative of opening up the clubs or conceding a ruff-and-discard.

You see why it would have been wrong to cash the last spade in the diagram position? What is declarer to throw from dummy? If a diamond, then West will take the ace on the first round and return the suit. If a club, then West will duck the first diamond, win the next, and play a third round, forcing South to ruff. In short, to play the spade before a diamond to the queen forces dummy to make a premature discard.

Example 18

Every textbook warns players not to double high contracts when the double may help to place the cards, but (fortunately for some) defenders still do it. It is especially unwise to double on the strength of trump tricks which are less than solid winners. Here is a typical example:

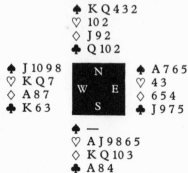

```
              ♠ K Q 4 3 2
              ♡ 10 2
              ◇ J 9 2
              ♣ Q 10 2
♠ J 10 9 8                    ♠ A 7 6 5
♡ K Q 7        N             ♡ 4 3
◇ A 8 7      W   E           ◇ 6 5 4
♣ K 6 3        S             ♣ J 9 7 5
              ♠ —
              ♡ A J 9 8 6 5
              ◇ K Q 10 3
              ♣ A 8 4
```

With both sides vulnerable, the bidding went:

SOUTH	WEST	NORTH	EAST
1 ♡	pass	1 ♠	pass
2 ◇	pass	2 ♡	pass
4 ♡	dble	pass	pass
pass			

West may have noted that North was a little unhappy about his false preference to two hearts, and that South was not too confident when he leapt to four hearts, but, even so, his double was unwise.

When the jack of spades was covered by the queen and ace at trick one, it became very clear that West's double must include at least K Q x of hearts. Taking advantage of this, South can make the contract in several ways. For example, he can lead a low club at trick two and use all entries to the table to ruff spades, reducing himself to A J 9 of trumps at the finish. This line depends on finding West with particular distribution, and South's order of play perhaps gave him more chances.

Having ruffed the first trick, he led a diamond to the nine discarded a club on the king of spades, and ruffed a spade. The king of diamonds was ducked; West took the next round and exited with a spade, which South ruffed. The position was now:

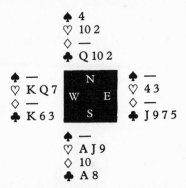

```
              ♠ 4
              ♡ 10 2
              ◇ —
              ♣ Q 10 2
  ♠ —          ┌─────────┐    ♠ —
  ♡ K Q 7      │    N    │    ♡ 4 3
  ◇ —          │ W     E │    ◇ —
  ♣ K 6 3      │    S    │    ♣ J 9 7 5
              └─────────┘
              ♠ —
              ♡ A J 9
              ◇ 10
              ♣ A 8
```

South led his thirteenth diamond, and it is obvious that West is
going to make only two more tricks. If he ruffs with the queen of
hearts, he will have to give up a trick in clubs or trumps with his
next lead, and if he discards a club, South will ruff with the ten of
hearts and play ace and another club.

Example 19

The next hand illustrates two principles: the first, very familiar by now, is that finesses should be postponed; the second, that when there is a choice of discards on a winner in dummy, the discard should not be taken early on, especially when the winner is part of a major tenace (such as A Q).

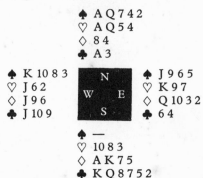

```
              ♠ A Q 7 4 2
              ♡ A Q 5 4
              ◇ 8 4
              ♣ A 3
 ♠ K 10 8 3                    ♠ J 9 6 5
 ♡ J 6 2         N             ♡ K 9 7
 ◇ J 9 6     W       E         ◇ Q 10 3 2
 ♣ J 10 9        S             ♣ 6 4
              ♠ —
              ♡ 10 8 3
              ◇ A K 7 5
              ♣ K Q 8 7 5 2
```

South plays in six clubs, and West leads the jack of clubs, won by dummy's ace.

Assuming a 3–2 break in trumps, declarer can count six clubs, four top winners in the side suits, and, barring accidents, a diamond ruff on the table. That adds up to eleven tricks. Obviously, a successful heart finesse would produce a twelfth, and a slight additional chance is to drop the king of spades in three rounds.

With the idea of combining these chances, South might begin with the ace and another spade, three rounds of diamonds, and another spade ruff. If the king of spades has not appeared, he can draw trumps and hope for a heart finesse or an end-play. Since East holds the king of hearts and the thirteenth diamond, he is exposed to a throw-in, but a good player would make the declarer guess by keeping at the finish the king of hearts alone, a diamond and a spade.

There is a somewhat better way of managing the hand. South should take the diamond ruff, enter hand by ruffing a low spade, and draw trumps. This brings him to:

1st July 2000

"Why miss an "even smaller extra chance?"

At TRICK TWO ruff a small spade in hand and THEN cash the top diamonds, followed by a small diamond ruffed in dummy. A second spade ruffed back in hand may just bring down a DOUBLETON KING (4·27%). Trumps are drawn in TWO ROUNDS, dummy's small heart being discarded. The KING of SPADES never appeared, NOW is the time to EXIT in diamonds.

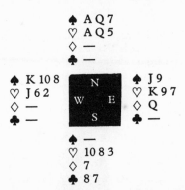

At this point South exits with his losing diamond. If West takes the trick, declarer will be at the mercy of the heart finesse, but if East wins, he will have to return a spade or a heart into dummy's major tenace. Note that this ending would not work if the ace of spades had been played off at an early stage.

Example 20

The theme of the next example is similar in one respect to the deal we have just been looking at. Declarer must not snatch at an early opportunity to discard on a winner in dummy, despite the fact that, superficially, there is no other entry to the table.

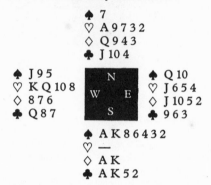

```
                    ♠ 7
                    ♡ A 9 7 3 2
                    ◇ Q 9 4 3
                    ♣ J 10 4
    ♠ J 9 5                        ♠ Q 10
    ♡ K Q 10 8      N              ♡ J 6 5 4
    ◇ 8 7 6      W     E           ◇ J 10 5 2
    ♣ Q 8 7         S              ♣ 9 6 3
                    ♠ A K 8 6 4 3 2
                    ♡ —
                    ◇ A K
                    ♣ A K 5 2
```

South plays in six spades, and West leads the king of hearts. At first sight the lead appears to be beneficial: it gives declarer a chance to take a discard on the ace of hearts and then finesse the jack of clubs.

But after giving the matter a little thought, South should spurn the apparent gift and ruff in hand. He must assume that trumps are 3-2 and, if he can lose the trump trick to the player on his left, all his difficulties will disappear. After ruffing the heart, he cashes the ace and king of spades, the ace and king of diamonds, plays the ace of clubs (in case there is a singleton queen anywhere), and exits in spades. This is the situation when West takes the spade trick:

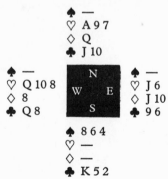

```
                    ♠ —
                    ♡ A 9 7
                    ◇ Q
                    ♣ J 10
    ♠ —                          ♠ —
    ♡ Q 10 8        N            ♡ J 6
    ◇ 8          W     E         ◇ J 10
    ♣ Q 8           S            ♣ 9 6
                    ♠ 8 6 4
                    ♡ —
                    ◇ —
                    ♣ K 5 2
```

Now West must concede entry to the table and declarer will not need the club finesse.

Note that this sequence of play does not give up any chances as compared with winning the first heart in dummy and taking the club finesse at once. If East, instead of West, wins the third round of spades, he will be obliged to open up the clubs. The contract will fail only if East has the third spade and West the guarded queen of clubs, and nothing can be done about that.

Example 21

The next hand is a little deceptive. We surmise that it would be differently played by four grades of player.

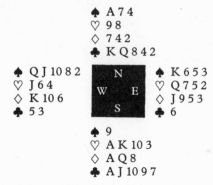

```
              ♠ A 7 4
              ♡ 9 8
              ◇ 7 4 2
              ♣ K Q 8 4 2
 ♠ Q J 10 8 2              ♠ K 6 5 3
 ♡ J 6 4          N        ♡ Q 7 5 2
 ◇ K 10 6     W       E    ◇ J 9 5 3
 ♣ 5 3            S        ♣ 6
              ♠ 9
              ♡ A K 10 3
              ◇ A Q 8
              ♣ A J 10 9 7
```

South is in six clubs, and West leads the queen of spades.

1) A beginner or moderate player would draw trumps and perhaps think of playing off ace, king, and another heart, in the hope of dropping the queen and jack in three rounds. When this failed, he would rest his fortunes on a finesse of the queen of diamonds.

2) A player with some understanding of elimination play would ruff out the spades and hearts and then, with only diamonds and clubs left, would play a low diamond from dummy towards the A Q 8. If East played low, declarer would put in the eight and make his contract, as West would have no good return; but it would not be difficult for East to foil this plan by putting in the nine of diamonds, preventing South from ducking the trick into West's hands.

3) A declarer more advanced in elimination technique would see possibilities in the heart suit. He would ruff out two spades and the third round of hearts and lead the fourth heart from hand. If West covered (having begun with Q x x x or J x x x or Q J x x), he would be allowed to hold the trick, South discarding a diamond from dummy in a typical loser-on-loser elimination. If West discarded on the fourth heart, South would ruff in dummy and lead a diamond towards the A Q 8, as before.

4) However, an expert who wanted to show off a little could claim the contract as soon as both opponents followed to the first round of trumps! He ruffs a spade at trick two, crosses to the king of clubs, ruffs another spade, and draws the second trump. Now he is on the table, with these cards remaining:

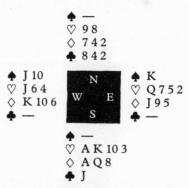

```
              ♠ —
              ♡ 9 8
              ◇ 7 4 2
              ♣ 8 4 2
  ♠ J 10                    ♠ K
  ♡ J 6 4      N            ♡ Q 7 5 2
  ◇ K 10 6   W   E          ◇ J 9 5
  ♣ —          S            ♣ —
              ♠ —
              ♡ A K 10 3
              ◇ A Q 8
              ♣ J
```

At this point South leads the eight of hearts from dummy and lets it
run! When West wins, he must either give up a trick in the red suits
or play a spade, conceding a ruff-and-discard. It would make no
difference, of course, if East, holding something like J x x of hearts,
were to cover the eight of hearts with the jack; South would win and
return a low heart to the nine, establishing the K 10 for two diamond
discards.

Easy to miss, wasn't it? Always look for opportunities to duck the
lead to a player who will have to play back into one of two major
tenaces, in this case A K 10 of hearts or A Q of diamonds. The same
idea was seen in Example 19.

Example 22

The usual style in textbooks is to proceed steadily from the easier hands to the more difficult. Nothing wrong with that—the present authors have done it many times—but it can also be useful to go back a little, as it were, from time to time. Here is a fairly routine exercise in loser-on-loser elimination. We think that, after quite a brief look at the diagram, you will see the winning line in four hearts.

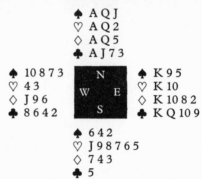

```
              ♠ A Q J
              ♡ A Q 2
              ◇ A Q 5
              ♣ A J 7 3
  ♠ 10 8 7 3      N       ♠ K 9 5
  ♡ 4 3                   ♡ K 10
  ◇ J 9 6    W       E    ◇ K 10 8 2
  ♣ 8 6 4 2      S        ♣ K Q 10 9
              ♠ 6 4 2
              ♡ J 9 8 7 6 5
              ◇ 7 4 3
              ♣ 5
```

North, with his balanced 24 points, opens two clubs, intending to rebid two no trumps, non-forcing in the Acol system. East can only pass over the two club opening, South gives a negative two diamonds, and North bids two no trumps, as planned. South bids three hearts and finally plays in four hearts. (This is not a treatise on bidding, but we may remark that an immediate four hearts over two no trumps is the best way to indicate a weak hand of this type; to bid three hearts and follow with four hearts over three no trumps suggests better values.)

West leads a spade against four hearts, and the dummy is a finesser's dream. But if South goes bald-headed for finesses in spades, hearts and diamonds, he will lose to the three kings and a second diamond as well. He will complain bitterly that East had all the strength, but this, in a way, should help him to make the contract.

The spade finesse must be taken at trick one, and East has nothing better than to return a spade. Declarer comes to hand with a club ruff and finesses the queen of hearts. East wins and returns a heart, won by dummy's ace. After another club ruff and a third round of spades the position is:

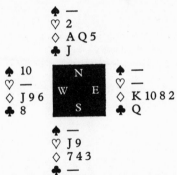

          ♠ —
          ♡ 2
          ◇ A Q 5
          ♣ J

♠ 10   ♠ —
♡ —   N   ♡ —
◇ J 9 6   W   E   ◇ K 10 8 2
♣ 8   S   ♣ Q

          ♠ —
          ♡ J 9
          ◇ 7 4 3
          ♣ —

Declarer leads the jack of clubs from dummy and is happy to see the
queen appear from East. This enables him to discard a diamond and
lay down his cards.

Example 23

To hold Q 10 x x of trumps over the A K J certainly provides
expectation of two trump tricks, and a defender who has already
made two tricks in the side suits against a contract of four hearts
may well feel optimistic. But he should not rejoice too soon, especially
if his adversary is a skilful player and if, like East on the deal below,
he has even distribution in the side suits.

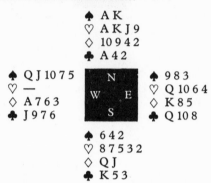

♠ A K
♡ A K J 9
◇ 10 9 4 2
♣ A 4 2

♠ Q J 10 7 5   ♠ 9 8 3
♡ —   ♡ Q 10 6 4
◇ A 7 6 3   ◇ K 8 5
♣ J 9 7 6   ♣ Q 10 8

♠ 6 4 2
♡ 8 7 5 3 2
◇ Q J
♣ K 5 3

South is in four hearts, and West leads the queen of spades. A round
of trumps discloses the bad news. It looks as though there are two
losers in hearts and two in diamonds, but South need not despair.

First, he must get a diamond trick going for a club discard. He plays
a diamond to the queen, and West switches to clubs. South wins with
the king and leads the jack of diamonds. He wins the next club in
dummy and takes his discard on the ten of diamonds, arriving at this
position:

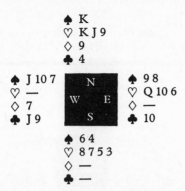

```
            ♠ K
            ♡ K J 9
            ◇ 9
            ♣ 4
♠ J 10 7              ♠ 9 8
♡ —       N          ♡ Q 10 6
◇ 7     W   E        ◇ —
♣ J 9     S          ♣ 10
            ♠ 6 4
            ♡ 8 7 5 3
            ◇ —
            ♣ —
```

Taking care to play his cards in the right order, South cashes the king of spades, ruffs a club, and ruffs a spade. Then he leads the nine of diamonds from dummy, and East, who has only Q 10 6 of hearts left, is end-played.

To bring about this type of ending the declarer generally needs to find the defender with a specific distribution. If East had held, say, a club less and a spade more, he would have been able to nip in with the ten of hearts on the third round of clubs.

Example 24

'Let George do it' is not a bad maxim to follow when you are playing a hand that contains a number of finesse positions. See if you can determine the right sequence to play on this hand:

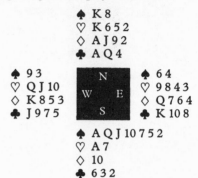

♠ K 8
♡ K 6 5 2
◇ A J 9 2
♣ A Q 4

♠ 9 3
♡ Q J 10
◇ K 8 5 3
♣ J 9 7 5

♠ 6 4
♡ 9 8 4 3
◇ Q 7 6 4
♣ K 10 8

♠ A Q J 10 7 5 2
♡ A 7
◇ 10
♣ 6 3 2

South deals and opens one spade, as he has too many high cards for a pre-emptive call. North has the values for a jump to three diamonds, but the modern style is to proceed more slowly on balanced hands. North bids simply two diamonds, therefore, and South makes a jump rebid of three spades. North might go through the motions of Blackwood, but seven is unlikely to be lay-down, so he goes directly to six spades.

The queen of hearts is led, and South can count eleven top tricks. Which way should he go for the twelfth?

Before resorting to the club finesse, declarer might be able to do something with the diamonds. He could win the heart lead in hand, draw trumps, play a diamond to the ace, and ruff a low diamond. If an honour appears on this trick, the contract is safe; declarer can enter dummy with the king of hearts, lead the jack of diamonds, and discard a club (unless East follows with the remaining honour in diamonds). The second club will then go away on the nine of diamonds.

There is a stronger line, however. If you have not seen it yet, look at Example 21 again, and see if that puts you on the right track.

Quite so! You eliminate the hearts, then run the ten of diamonds, leaving East on play.

But be sure to leave yourself with enough entries to ruff out the hearts. After just one round of trumps, you must take the very slight risk of leading a heart to the king. If this stands up, you ruff a heart, cross to the king of spades, and ruff the fourth heart. The position is then:

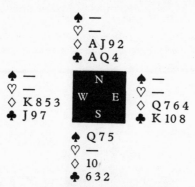

```
                    ♠ —
                    ♡ —
                    ◇ A J 9 2
                    ♣ A Q 4
    ♠ —          ┌─────────┐         ♠ —
    ♡ —          │    N    │         ♡ —
    ◇ K 8 5 3    │ W     E │         ◇ Q 7 6 4
    ♣ J 9 7      │    S    │         ♣ K 10 8
                 └─────────┘
                    ♠ Q 7 5
                    ♡ —
                    ◇ 10
                    ♣ 6 3 2
```

Now you lead the ten of diamonds and, if West plays low, you let the
ten run. All the hearts have gone, so you know that East, after
winning the diamond trick, will be forced to lead up to one of the
tenaces in dummy. That is what we mean when we say 'Let George
do it'.

Should West cover the ten of diamonds with the king or queen, you
simply win with the ace and return the jack, intending to discard one
club on the jack of diamonds and one on the nine.

Example 25

Elimination play is often combined with 'dummy reversal'. A player is said to reverse the dummy when he takes ruffs in his own hand to the point when dummy's trumps become longer than his own and are used to draw those of the opponents. To put it another way, dummy becomes the master hand.

```
                    ♠ A Q 10 4
                    ♡ Q 5 4
                    ◇ K Q 8
                    ♣ A Q 10
     ♠ 9 8 5 3                      ♠ K J 7 2
     ♡ 7 3            N             ♡ J 10 8 6
     ◇ 6 4 2      W       E        ◇ 5 3
     ♣ 9 7 4 2        S             ♣ K J 5
                    ♠ 6
                    ♡ A K 9 2
                    ◇ A J 10 9 7
                    ♣ 8 6 3
```

South is in six diamonds and West leads the nine of spades. There are only ten tricks on top, and the spade finesse does not look promising after the lead.

On the surface, there are only five tricks in diamonds, but declarer can increase the trick-winning power of the trump suit by ruffing three spades in hand and using dummy's K Q 8 to draw the opponents trumps.

With this plan in mind, declarer wins the first trick with the ace of spades, ruffs a spade, crosses to the queen of hearts and ruffs another spade. After a diamond to the queen, the fourth spade is ruffed with the ace of diamonds, and South plays his last trump to dummy. The reverse-dummy procedure has gone well, and the position is:

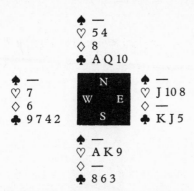

♠ —
♡ 5 4
◊ 8
♣ A Q 10

♠ —
♡ 7
◊ 6
♣ 9 7 4 2

N
W   E
S

♠ —
♡ J 10 8
◊ —
♣ K J 5

♠ —
♡ A K 9
◊ —
♣ 8 6 3

The last trump is drawn from dummy; East discards a club, and so does South. When the ace and king of hearts are played off, it becomes apparent that East has the long heart. As East's spades and diamonds have been eliminated, declarer can exit with the last heart in the knowledge that East will be forced to return a club into dummy's A Q.

Example 26

Most of the elimination plays we have looked at have been designed to obviate the need for a finesse. Sometimes, in a trump contract, the finesse element is not present at all. Declarer makes an extra trick by forcing the defender to concede a ruff-and-discard.

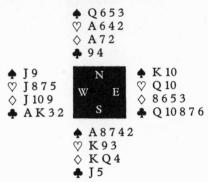

```
                ♠ Q 6 5 3
                ♡ A 6 4 2
                ◇ A 7 2
                ♣ 9 4
  ♠ J 9            N          ♠ K 10
  ♡ J 8 7 5                   ♡ Q 10
  ◇ J 10 9     W      E       ◇ 8 6 5 3
  ♣ A K 3 2        S          ♣ Q 10 8 7 6
                ♠ A 8 7 4 2
                ♡ K 9 3
                ◇ K Q 4
                ♣ J 5
```

South opens one spade, North raises to three spades, and South, slightly against his better judgement, perhaps, bids the game. West cashes two club tricks and switches to the jack of diamonds.

The hands do not fit well, both players holding a doubleton in the same suit, and prospects are poor. At least one trump trick must be lost however the suit is divided, and there is no obvious way to avoid the loss of a heart. There is only one chance: to lose the second round of trumps to a player who will be compelled to allow a ruff-and-discard.

South lays down the ace of spades, but does not play a second round until he has eliminated the diamonds and taken two rounds of hearts. After everyone has followed to the ace and king of hearts and two more rounds of diamonds, the position is:

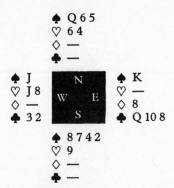

```
              ♠ Q 6 5
              ♡ 6 4
              ◊ —
              ♣ —
    ♠ J            N          ♠ K
    ♡ J 8     W        E      ♡ —
    ◊ —                       ◊ 8
    ♣ 3 2          S          ♣ Q 10 8
              ♠ 8 7 4 2
              ♡ 9
              ◊ —
              ♣ —
```

South is in luck, for when he exits with a trump, not only does he find the spades 1-1 but the player with the king has no more hearts to lead. This is a pure ruff-and-discard elimination.

Example 27

Sometimes it is clear that a successful elimination will win the contract however the cards lie; sometimes declarer has to hope for a particular distribution. Thus, in the last hand we looked at, South played for one of the defenders to hold a doubleton in spades and a doubleton heart.

It is a good mental approach, when it is clear that a contract can be made only if the cards lie in such and such a way, to assume that they do so lie and to play confidently on that basis. And there is a further stage in this: when the contract would be simple if one suit broke well, assume that it breaks poorly and consider what chances are left.

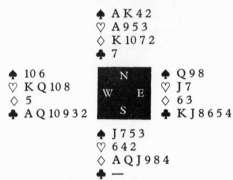

```
              ♠ A K 4 2
              ♡ A 9 5 3
              ◇ K 10 7 2
              ♣ 7
♠ 10 6                        ♠ Q 9 8
♡ K Q 10 8      N            ♡ J 7
◇ 5           W   E          ◇ 6 3
♣ A Q 10 9 3 2    S          ♣ K J 8 6 5 4
              ♠ J 7 5 3
              ♡ 6 4 2
              ◇ A Q J 9 8 4
              ♣ —
```

West opens one club, North doubles, and East attempts to shut out the opposition with a leap to five clubs. South is too strong, however, and his bid of five diamonds buys the contract.

West leads the king of hearts, and South finds himself in the type of situation we outlined above. If the spades are lucky—a doubleton queen falling—the contract will present no difficulty. South should assume, therefore, that the queen is twice guarded. If that is the case, the only chance will lie in a ruff-and-discard elimination. South will need to find the same opponent with Q x x of spades and a doubleton heart.

Having reasoned along these lines, declarer ducks the first round of hearts. West will probably lay down the ace of clubs, which South will ruff. After two rounds of trumps, declarer plays off the ace and king of spades arriving at this position:

the suit from West's hand.

South's last diamond was ruffed in DUMMY clearing the DIAMONDS from WEST's hand.

```
                    SPADES J,5
                    HEARTS 10,8
                    DIAMONDS VOID
                    CLUBS 9                    SPADES 9,8,6,4
SPADES K,10,7,3                                HEARTS J
HEARTS VOID                                    DIAMONDS VOID
DIAMONDS VOID                                  CLUBS VOID
CLUBS K
                    SPADES A,Q,2
                    HEARTS VOID
                    DIAMONDS VOID
                    CLUBS Q
```

NOW a heart is led from dummy (establishing [it]) and ruffed in hand. What [ ] clearer? If WEST overruffs he is [ ]ld and if he discards a SPADE, [ ] lears trumps and endplays him all at [ ]

30th June, 2000

AT TRICK 3 it occurred to me: the general idea must be to END PLAY WEST with the KING OF TROMPS after the RED SUITS had been eliminated. However, because WEST had bid DIAMONDS it seemed necessary to eliminate that suit first (just to be on the safe side).

Instead of ruffing a heart I crossed to the ACE OF TRUMPS IN HAND and at TRICK 4 I ruffed a low diamond. Now I ruffed a HEART back in hand. A second diamond was ruffed in dummy at TRICK 6, followed by a heart ruffed back in hand; idea

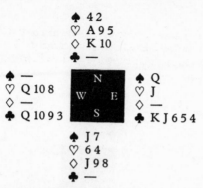

```
            ♠ 4 2
            ♡ A 9 5
            ◇ K 10
            ♣ —
♠ —                         ♠ Q
♡ Q 10 8    ┌─────────┐    ♡ J
◇ —         │    N    │    ◇ —
♣ Q 10 9 3  │ W     E │    ♣ K J 6 5 4
            │    S    │
            └─────────┘
            ♠ J 7
            ♡ 6 4
            ◇ J 9 8
            ♣ —
```

Now South cashes the ace of hearts and exits with a spade, leaving
East on play.

Example 28

Many forms of play are highly interesting in a technical sense, although it must be admitted that they seldom occur in play. The deal below comes into that category. You will certainly find it both elegant and surprising.

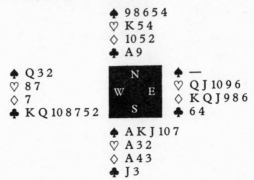

```
                    ♠ 9 8 6 5 4
                    ♡ K 5 4
                    ◇ 10 5 2
                    ♣ A 9
  ♠ Q 3 2            ┌─────────┐           ♠ —
  ♡ 8 7              │    N    │           ♡ Q J 10 9 6
  ◇ 7                │ W     E │           ◇ K Q J 9 8 6
  ♣ K Q 10 8 7 5 2   │    S    │           ♣ 6 4
                    └─────────┘
                    ♠ A K J 10 7
                    ♡ A 3 2
                    ◇ A 4 3
                    ♣ J 3
```

South opens one spade; West, playing weak jump overcalls, bids three clubs; and North supports his partner to three spades. East ventures four diamonds, and South's four spades buys the contract.

West leads the king of clubs, and dummy wins. A round of trumps marks West with Q x x.

South is now looking at five losers—one in spades, one in hearts, two in diamonds, and one in clubs. He reduces them to three by a very pretty coup.

First, he cashes the top winners in the red suits; then he plays off a second trump, followed by the jack of clubs. West has the lead, and the remaining cards are:

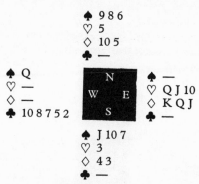

```
              ♠ 9 8 6
              ♡ 5
              ◇ 10 5
              ♣ —
♠ Q                       ♠ —
♡ —        N              ♡ Q J 10
◇ —      W   E            ◇ K Q J
♣ 10 8 7 5 2  S           ♣ —
              ♠ J 10 7
              ♡ 3
              ◇ 4 3
              ♣ —
```

West cashes the queen of spades and leads a club, giving South the chance for a ruff-and-discard. But South has a different plan in mind: instead of ruffing, he discards a heart from dummy and a diamond from his own hand. When West, still in the lead, plays another club, South ruffs in dummy and discards his remaining diamond. Now he makes the rest of the tricks by a cross-ruff. This is a 'double-discard elimination'.

One interesting point: South must give West the lead with the queen of clubs, not the queen of spades. If the spade is played first, West may make the sparkling play of underleading the queen of clubs. South makes the jack but is left with three losers in the red suits.

Example 29

Quite often a declarer will find that there are two ways of playing a
suit: he may be able to choose between a simple finesse and a ruff-
and-discard elimination.

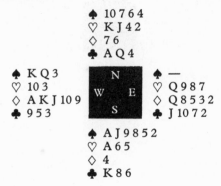

```
              ♠ 10 7 6 4
              ♡ K J 4 2
              ◇ 7 6
              ♣ A Q 4
  ♠ K Q 3        N         ♠ —
  ♡ 10 3                   ♡ Q 9 8 7
  ◇ A K J 10 9  W    E     ◇ Q 8 5 3 2
  ♣ 9 5 3          S       ♣ J 10 7 2
              ♠ A J 9 8 5 2
              ♡ A 6 5
              ◇ 4
              ♣ K 8 6
```

The bidding goes:

SOUTH	WEST	NORTH	EAST
1 ♠	2 ◇	3 ♠	4 ◇
4 ♠	pass	pass	pass

West wins the first trick with the king of diamonds and follows with
the ace of diamonds, which South ruffs.

To play off the ace of spades would be a slight error, because East
might hold K Q x and West a void. South crosses to dummy with a
club, therefore, to lead a low spade, intending to put in the jack if
East plays low. When East shows out, however, declarer goes up
with the ace.

Two spades and a diamond are now certain losers. An unthinking
player would conclude that the contract depended on the heart
finesse, and when this lost he would blame the fates, commenting on
the 3-0 break in spades and the position of the queen of hearts.

Instead of committing himself to the heart finesse, South should
consider the possibility of a ruff-and-discard elimination. This will
depend on West holding a doubleton heart. To improve his count of
the West hand South plays off two more rounds of clubs, discovering
that West began with at least three clubs. These cards are left:

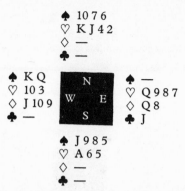

```
            ♠ 10 7 6
            ♡ K J 4 2
            ◇ —
            ♣ —

♠ K Q         ┌─────────┐       ♠ —
♡ 10 3        │    N    │       ♡ Q 9 8 7
◇ J 10 9      │ W     E │       ◇ Q 8
♣ —           │    S    │       ♣ J
              └─────────┘
            ♠ J 9 8 5
            ♡ A 6 5
            ◇ —
            ♣ —
```

South cannot see the West cards but he can be sure that West, who has turned up with three spades and three clubs and must have five diamonds for his overcall, does not hold more than two hearts. The right line, therefore, is to cash ace and king of hearts, then throw the lead in spades, forcing West to concede a ruff-and-discard.

Example 30

Many hands that call for elimination play, while not particularly difficult, are both amusing and instructive. South appears to have two losers on the deal below, but one of them disappears as if by magic.

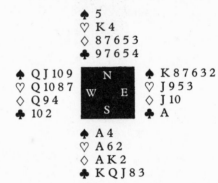

```
                    ♠ 5
                    ♡ K 4
                    ◇ 8 7 6 5 3
                    ♣ 9 7 6 5 4
        ♠ Q J 10 9      N        ♠ K 8 7 6 3 2
        ♡ Q 10 8 7   W      E    ♡ J 9 5 3
        ◇ Q 9 4                  ◇ J 10
        ♣ 10 2          S        ♣ A
                    ♠ A 4
                    ♡ A 6 2
                    ◇ A K 2
                    ♣ K Q J 8 3
```

South opened with a restrained one club and did a lot of 'catching up' afterwards. North raised to two clubs, South bid two diamonds (forcing), and North three clubs. When South tried three hearts, North felt justified in going to five clubs, and South, with little justification, advanced to six clubs. West led the queen of spades.

South appears to have two losers, one in clubs and one in diamonds, and there is no chance of a squeeze. There is only one possibility— that the same hand will have a singleton ace of clubs and a doubleton diamond.

After winning with the ace of spades, South ruffed a spade, eliminated the hearts by ruffing the third round, and cashed ace and king of diamonds. Then he exited with a trump and a prayer. When East won with the ace of clubs, the position was:

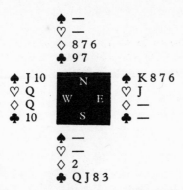

```
              ♠ —
              ♡ —
              ◇ 8 7 6
              ♣ 9 7
  ♠ J 10                    ♠ K 8 7 6
  ♡ Q         N             ♡ J
  ◇ Q      W     E          ◇ —
  ♣ 10        S             ♣ —
              ♠ —
              ♡ —
              ◇ 2
              ♣ Q J 8 3
```

East had to lead a major suit, and South was able to dispose of his diamond loser.

An opening club lead would have beaten this contract, but West cannot be blamed for leading from his strong sequence in spades. As often happens, the singleton ace of trumps proved to be a liability in defence.

Example 31

When a declarer executes a throw-in, he usually aims to lose the trick to a particular opponent. An odd feature of the deal below was that when South gave up the third round of spades he was confident that whichever opponent won the trick would be obliged to concede a ruff-and-discard.

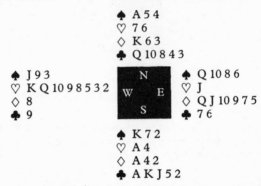

```
                    ♠ A 5 4
                    ♡ 7 6
                    ◇ K 6 3
                    ♣ Q 10 8 4 3
      ♠ J 9 3                          ♠ Q 10 8 6
      ♡ K Q 10 9 8 5 3 2               ♡ J
      ◇ 8                              ◇ Q J 10 9 7 5
      ♣ 9                              ♣ 7 6
                    ♠ K 7 2
                    ♡ A 4
                    ◇ A 4 2
                    ♣ A K J 5 2
```

South opened one club, West overcalled with four hearts, and North, who had an awkward choice between double and five clubs, chose to support his partner. South, with 19 points and three aces, must have been tempted to bid six, but he realized that his partner might have been forced to stretch and showed good judgement in passing five clubs.

West led the king of hearts, and the declarer won. As is usually the case when both players (declarer and dummy) have identical distribution, there were more losers than one would expect with so many high cards.

It was obviously a hand for elimination play, so declarer drew trumps and cashed the top winners in spades and diamonds, arriving at this position:

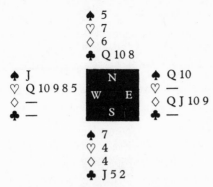

                    ♠ 5
                    ♡ 7
                    ◇ 6
                    ♣ Q 10 8
    ♠ J   ♠ Q 10
    ♡ Q 10 9 8 5   N   ♡ —
    ◇ —   W   E   ◇ Q J 10 9
    ♣ —   S   ♣ —
                    ♠ 7
                    ♡ 4
                    ◇ 4
                    ♣ J 5 2

It was necessary to exit with a spade now, to limit communication
between the defending hands. Whichever opponent wins this trick
can cash one further winner but must then concede a ruff-and-discard.

Note that in the diagram position it is insufficient to exit with either a
heart or a diamond. If South plays a diamond, for example, East can
defeat the contract by underleading his queen of spades.

Example 32

The next hand illustrates a very important and quite common form of elimination play. A defender is unable to attack a suit because, if he does so, he creates a finesse position against himself. Observe the club suit below. If West captures the queen with the ace, he cannot return the suit without abandoning his second trick.

South is in four hearts, and West leads the queen of spades. Declarer draws trumps in three rounds, then plays a club from dummy to the queen and ace. West exits with the jack of spades to dummy's king. This is the situation now:

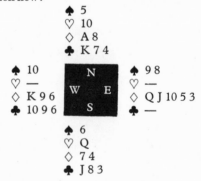

South has lost only one trick, and the contract is certain so long as he does not play another round of clubs. He can simply play the ace and another diamond. The defenders take a diamond and a spade. If East is then on lead, he must concede a ruff-and-discard, while if West has the lead, he cannot play another club without exposing himself to a finesse.

It would have made no difference if West had refused to win the queen of clubs earlier on. As the cards lie, South can play a second club to the king, then execute the same elimination. But it would be better play (because East might possibly have held A 10 9 5 of clubs) to exit at once in diamonds or spades. Once again, if the opponents have to lead clubs when dummy has K x x and declarer J x x , only one club trick will be lost.

Example 33

The next hand belongs to the same family as the one above. If he attacks the club suit himself, South will lose a trick to East's J 10 x x; by forcing the opponents to play the suit (or to concede a ruff-and-discard) he escapes the loser.

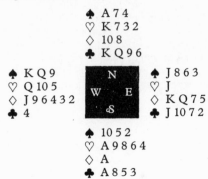

```
                    ♠ A 7 4
                    ♡ K 7 3 2
                    ◇ 10 8
                    ♣ K Q 9 6
   ♠ K Q 9                      ♠ J 8 6 3
   ♡ Q 10 5          N          ♡ J
   ◇ J 9 6 4 3 2  W    E        ◇ K Q 7 5
   ♣ 4              S           ♣ J 10 7 2
                    ♠ 10 5 2
                    ♡ A 9 8 6 4
                    ◇ A
                    ♣ A 8 5 3
```

South is in four hearts, and West, having a likely trump trick, opens the king of spades in preference to the singleton club. Declarer takes the trick in dummy, plays a heart to the ace, cashes the ace of diamonds, and plays a second heart to the king, finding that he must lose a trump trick. Following general principles, he eliminates the second diamond, and the position is now:

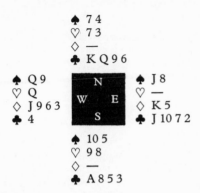

```
              ♠ 7 4
              ♡ 7 3
              ♢ —
              ♣ K Q 9 6
  ♠ Q 9                      ♠ J 8
  ♡ Q          N             ♡ —
  ♢ J 9 6 3   W   E          ♢ K 5
  ♣ 4          S             ♣ J 10 7 2
              ♠ 10 5
              ♡ 9 8
              ♢ —
              ♣ A 8 5 3
```

At this point South must play accurately. Suppose he exits
prematurely with a trump or a spade. West will make two spades and
a heart, then lead his singleton club, and South will have to lose a club
trick eventually.

In the diagram position South must first lead a club to the king; only
then does he exit in spades or trumps. Now, however the clubs lie,
South will lose no tricks in the suit. West has no club to lead, and if
East plays from the J 10 7, he will be open to a finesse on the next
round.

Example 34

Still on the theme of what may be thought of as elimination plays within a single suit, there are many combinations where the best technique is to begin with a low card from hand. Imagine a suit to be distributed in one of the following ways:

10 5 4

K J 7 3   Q

A 6 2

West has overcalled in this suit and has made two discards from it. Since he did not lead the suit, it is certain that he does not hold K Q J If he has eliminated the other suits and still has trumps in both hands South can hold the losers to one by exiting with a low card. If West takes the trick, he will have to lead back into a tenace, and if East wins, he will be obliged to concede a ruff-and-discard.

A 8 4 2

Q 10 9 3   J

K 7 6 5

This is a side suit, and again declarer has trumps in both hands and has eliminated the other suits. If he plays off ace and king, he loses two tricks. A low card from both hands is surprisingly effective. Suppose the lead is in dummy and the play goes 2, J, 5: West must either leave his partner on play or overtake with the queen and surrender a trick with his next lead.

With these examples in mind you will have no difficulty in finding the right play on this deal:

♠ K 7 5 3
♡ A
◇ K Q 8 4
♣ 10 7 5 2

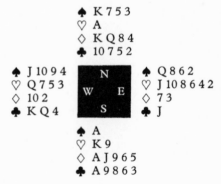

♠ J 10 9 4   ♠ Q 8 6 2
♡ Q 7 5 3   ♡ J 10 8 6 4 2
◇ 10 2   ◇ 7 3
♣ K Q 4   ♣ J

♠ A
♡ K 9
◇ A J 9 6 5
♣ A 9 8 6 3

South plays in six diamonds, and West leads the jack of spades.
Taking care with his entries, South draws trumps and eliminates the
spades and hearts, arriving at this position:

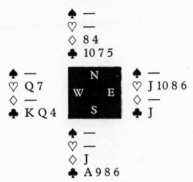

South can do better than play off ace and another club, hoping for a
2-2 break. Instead, he leads a low club and the opponents find
themselves in the familiar dilemma.

Example 35

One good end-play is worth more than two bad finesses. That is the lesson of the following hand:

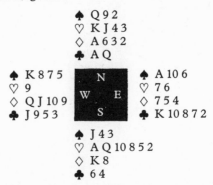

```
              ♠ Q 9 2
              ♡ K J 4 3
              ◇ A 6 3 2
              ♣ A Q
  ♠ K 8 7 5      N        ♠ A 10 6
  ♡ 9                     ♡ 7 6
  ◇ Q J 10 9   W   E      ◇ 7 5 4
  ♣ J 9 5 3      S        ♣ K 10 8 7 2
              ♠ J 4 3
              ♡ A Q 10 8 5 2
              ◇ K 8
              ♣ 6 4
```

West leads the queen of diamonds against South's contract of four hearts. Declarer wins with the king and draws trumps in two rounds.

There are finesse positions in spades and in clubs, but if declarer takes them both, he will lose the contract. If he begins by finessing the queen of clubs, East wins and returns a club to dummy's ace. South now plays a spade to the jack and king. Later, he tries a finesse of the nine of spades, but this, too, proves 'unlucky'.

As any player knows who has played the game for more than a few weeks, the combination of Q x x opposite J x x (even without the nine) represents a certain trick *so long as the opponents make the first lead of the suit*. Bearing this in mind, South, who can afford to lose one club and two spades, should plan an elimination.

After drawing trumps, he plays a diamond to the ace and ruffs a diamond, enters dummy with the ace of clubs, spurning the finesse, and ruffs the last diamond. He is then in this happy position:

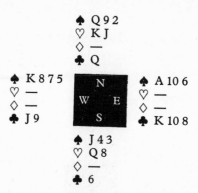

South plays a club to the queen and king, and East has to open up the spades.

Needless to say, if South had to make eleven tricks on this deal, he would take the club finesse and subsequently the spade finesse. Playing in four hearts, he makes sure of his contract by refusing the club finesse and keeping the queen as a card of exit.

Example 36

The possibility of gaining a trick through elimination play often
influences the declarer when he has a close choice between playing
for the drop in the trump suit or taking a finesse. Sometimes the
situation is that if he takes the finesse and loses he will at once regain
the trick.

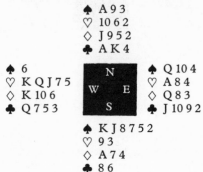

```
                    ♠ A 9 3
                    ♡ 10 6 2
                    ◇ J 9 5 2
                    ♣ A K 4
    ♠ 6                           ♠ Q 10 4
    ♡ K Q J 7 5        N          ♡ A 8 4
    ◇ K 10 6       W      E       ◇ Q 8 3
    ♣ Q 7 5 3          S          ♣ J 10 9 2
                    ♠ K J 8 7 5 2
                    ♡ 9 3
                    ◇ A 7 4
                    ♣ 8 6
```

South is in three spades, and the defenders begin with the king,
queen, and another heart, South ruffing the third round.

There are two potential losers in diamonds, and the contract
appears to depend on catching the queen of spades. Other things
being equal, there is a slight percentage in favour of playing for the
drop with nine cards. However, there is a tactical point in the hand.
South's best line is to eliminate the clubs, play a spade to the ace, and
finesse the jack on the way back. As the cards lie, that wins the
contract without further effort.

But suppose, instead, that West had held Q x of spades and a club
less. The trump finesse would lose, and the position would be:

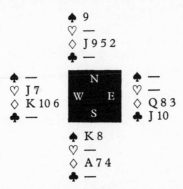

West is on lead and must open up the diamonds, giving South a good chance to save a trick in this suit. If West led a low diamond, declarer would put in the nine, forcing the queen and ace, and would lose only one trick. An expert defender in West's position, knowing that two diamond tricks were needed, would exit with the king.

South would win with the ace and return a diamond; when West played low, declarer would have to decide whether to put in the nine or the jack.

The elimination play is not a sure thing here, but the extra chances it provides are sufficient to make the trump finesse the correct play.

Example 37

In most of the examples in this book we have shown hands where the declarer, after drawing trumps and eliminating side suits, has been in the comfortable position of having trumps left in each hand. It must be said, however, that at the table it is often not possible to draw all the opposing trumps and remain with at least one trump in each hand. This does not mean that the elimination idea should necessarily be abandoned. Declarer may have reason to hope that the player who is thrown in will not hold the missing trump.

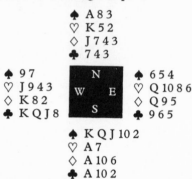

```
                 ♠ A 8 3
                 ♡ K 5 2
                 ◇ J 7 4 3
                 ♣ 7 4 3
   ♠ 9 7           N           ♠ 6 5 4
   ♡ J 9 4 3    W     E        ♡ Q 10 8 6
   ◇ K 8 2         S           ◇ Q 9 5
   ♣ K Q J 8                   ♣ 9 6 5
                 ♠ K Q J 10 2
                 ♡ A 7
                 ◇ A 10 6
                 ♣ A 10 2
```

South plays in four spades against the lead of the king of clubs. Prospects are not too good because he is threatened with the loss of two clubs and two diamonds. He might, it is true, keep the diamond losses to one by finding East with K Q or even with a doubleton Q x or K x, but he would certainly prefer the opponents to open up the suit.

At first sight, an elimination play may not appear to be practicable, because declarer cannot draw trumps and remain with a trump in each hand. To play three rounds of spades, eliminate the hearts, and exit in clubs, would achieve nothing, as the opponents would not be obliged to play diamonds.

But perhaps two rounds of trumps will extract those of the opponent who is to be thrown in. As his idea is to end-play West, South holds off the first club, wins the second, and draws just two rounds of trumps with the king and queen. Three rounds of hearts eliminate this suit, and the position is as follows:

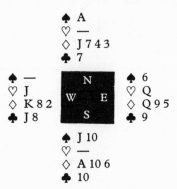

```
                ♠ A
                ♡ —
                ◇ J 7 4 3
                ♣ 7
  ♠ —                      ♠ 6
  ♡ J          N           ♡ Q
  ◇ K 8 2   W     E        ◇ Q 9 5
  ♣ J 8         S          ♣ 9
                ♠ J 10
                ♡ —
                ◇ A 10 6
                ♣ 10
```

South exits with the ten of clubs to West's jack. Now a heart or club from West allows a ruff-and-discard, and a diamond solves all problems in that suit.

It was, of course, necessary to find West with only two trumps, for if he had held the outstanding trump, he would have been able to exit safely. The declarer's good luck was earned by his good technique.